Keeping A Spiritual Journal

D1711352

KEEPING A SPIRITUAL JOURNAL

HARRY J.
CARGAS

ROGER J.
RADLEY

NAZARETH BOOKS™
Doubleday & Company, Inc.
Garden City, New York

Nazareth Books is a trademark of Catholic Heritage Press, Inc.

Project Directors for Nazareth Books ™

John J. Kirvan

Roger J. Radley

ISBN: 0-385-17439-X
Library of Congress Catalog Card Number: 80-2072

Contents

Contents

Chapter 1
Opening Up

In this time of Space Lab and the exploring of outer space, of *Star Wars* and *Star Trek,* there are people who spend their lives planning intergalactic journeys. Some few people have already been in space, walked on the moon, and returned to share their experiences through books, movies, and TV appearances. Scientists discuss unknown galaxies as if they were across the street rather than light-years away.

At the same time, millions of other people are journeying into "inner space," the mysterious world that lies at the center of every human life. The vehicles for this journey seem to multiply with every season. Meditation, yoga, TM, *est*; various forms of psychology and therapy, philosophy and religion promise a safe and satisfying journey into the depths of our souls. And, like the travelers in outer space, there are those who claim to have found the center of life and its meaning, and they also share their discoveries with us through movies, books, and TV shows.

Maybe you have read one of those self-help books, or maybe your parents and friends have told you of them. There are hundreds to choose from. But the most important book for your journey into the mysteries of your life has not yet been written.

The most important book for you could be the book that only you can write—your own journal.

A journal is a book that you write about yourself. It can begin at any time, anywhere. You add to it day after day, but unlike other books, this book need not end before you want it to. No one except God knows the end of the story. And the story may change every day even as you change.

A journal is a book in which you keep a personal record of events in your life, of your different relationships, of your response to things, of your feelings about things—of your search to find out who you are and what the meaning of your life might be. It is a book in which you carry out the greatest of life's adventures—the discovery of yourself.

A journal, however, is not a diary, even though both are books in which you write each day. Your diary is a kind of history, a record of what you did and when you did it. *"Monday I went to the basketball game . . . Tuesday I got a C+ on my math test . . . Wednesday I asked Laura to the dance . . . Thursday not a darn thing happened . . . Friday I earned a part in the school play . . . Saturday I had to clean the garage . . . Sunday, after church, the whole family went on a picnic."* These are diary entries. The ones you make may be longer, but they have little to do with keeping a journal. These diary notations tell what and when, and sometimes how and why.

But a journal is about *who*—*who* the writer is—*who*

8

you are.

That doesn't necessarily mean that you will be able to sit down every day and write wonderful pages on who you are and have it all come out clear and exciting. You aren't like that. You are a mystery that can never be solved; it will take a long time, much effort, and much grace to come to know and appreciate the unique person you are.

A journal is about who you are because its purpose is to seek clues and answers to this great question. Each day it looks at your life in a quiet, steady way to uncover bit by bit the great mystery of your life. Some days you will understand what you have written. But what you write on other days may not be completely understood for years to come. Five years from now, or even ten, you will reread a page and discover for the first time the importance of what you are experiencing now.

This book will tell you how you can start and maintain the wonderful experience called a journal.

Still, we are not going to tell you how to keep a journal. You are going to discover for yourself how it is done by actually doing it. For the remainder of this book we will be suggesting a series of experiences to think about, questions to answer, and things to do and write that will help you enjoy the results that come from keeping a journal.

But we should stop for a moment and look ahead to some of the good things that our own journals can bring us.

Your journal can be a tool to help you listen to yourself and to find God right in your own life. No

9

journal will make you a saint, nor will it tell you exactly who God is. Your journal, however, can help you "keep on the beam." It can help you to choose those things that seem to bring you closer to yourself and the God that you understand from your daily life.

Your journal is a way of being good to yourself. The time you save for yourself each day to record experiences and feelings is a gift to yourself. A gift you deserve. It doesn't matter how you feel about God or yourself on any day; if you write in a journal, you are thinking well of yourself. Even when you think no one loves you, you'll know you care enough for yourself to give yourself this daily gift.

You can use your journal to work out how you feel about most anything (even things you cannot share with anyone else). Sometimes writing in your journal can give you a chance to decide not to act on the way you feel and can save you a lot of discomfort and pain later. Even when your journal doesn't tell you what to do, it helps you feel okay about not knowing what to do. A journal can help you live with, and understand, how you feel even when it hurts inside. (How sad it is when people think that the only good way to feel is happy, cheerful, and carefree!) Through your journal, you can discover that any feeling that helps you understand yourself better, or any feeling that helps you grow, is a good feeling for you. If being afraid helps you to discover what or whom frightens you, that may be good for you. If being afraid helps you discover that you have everything you need to have a good day today, then being afraid can be good for you.

Most important, keeping a journal can help us escape from the masks we wear. All of us wear masks and try to act as we think others want us to act. You might be one person to your mother, another to your friends at school, another to your enemies, another to your teacher, and still another to your grandmother or the lady down the street. We often behave differently depending on the roles we play. Do you speak the same way to your parents as you speak to your friends on the ball field? Do you talk to your mother and father the same way when they ask you to take out the garbage as when you want them to take you for a burger and fries?

When you feel that you are in love, you may know the situation is different, but not know what to say or do. You might even try one of your other roles or masks, one you think will work, only to have the other person walk away. Or you might not be able to say anything about your feelings to the other person and just feel afraid and discouraged.

Masks, roles, playing, acting is not always bad. Everyone uses these to fit comfortably in certain situations. In some sense, we are all actors. Could you imagine the confusion if:

> you spoke to your mom the same way you did to your friend who threw your gym clothes in the shower?

how about:

> dressing for school the same way you do for the beach or ski slopes?

We have lots of roles. Some we choose. Others we do not choose. Following is a brief list of some roles we automatically have:

1. an **American** (or Pole or Japanese or other)
2. a **woman** (or man)
3. a **Northerner** (or Easterner or Californian)
4. an **Indian** (or Caucasian, black, Oriental, or Hispanic)
5. a **parent** (or child or brother or sister)
6. a **consumer** (or seller or producer)
7. a **Democrat** (or Republican or anarchist or Conservative)
8. a **healthy person** (or one who is not well)
9. a **poor person** (or affluent or middle class or rich)
10. a **landlord** (or a tenant or landowner)
11. a **clerk** (or professor or truck driver)
12. a **student** (or dropout or teacher)

Where you live, your age, your family background, your health, the color of your skin, and even the amount of money you or your family have can and often do affect how you behave. But none of the items listed above, or the many others we could have listed, tell you or others who you are. To find that out, you have to shed all the masks. And a special tool to help you reach that kind of honesty is your journal.

What Do You Need to Make a Journal Work?

Because you have such high hopes for your journal, you will want to observe a few rules that will help keep your journal the place of discovery and growth that it can be.

Following are some suggested rules.

1. Keep It Honest

Many who find being honest with others difficult have found that a journal is a wonderful and necessary place to begin the practice of honesty. After all, there is no point in lying to yourself or hiding from yourself. Jesus has stressed that "the truth shall make you free." Jesus knew that it would not be easy. Often it seems we are punished for honesty. But being honest with yourself is its own reward. So don't write what you would like to be the truth.

Don't write something you think your parents or friends or teachers might like you to feel and say. Write honestly about yourself. Write for yourself.

2. Make a Plan

Journal keeping is a tool to make your life better. Set a time of day and length of time. Write a contract in your journal:

Every day (every other day) I will write in my journal at ____o'clock for at least ____hour. I will write in my journal because it is my gift

to me, and I deserve this gift.

Some days you may decide not to write. The next day, or later on when you do write in your journal, try writing about why you didn't write at your regular time. Talk about what else you did and how it helped you be more you.

Besides setting a particular time to write, it is a good idea to choose a place that will give you quiet and space to be alone. A place in which you feel comfortable and able to write honestly about yourself is what you need.

Some days it will be easier to write than others, but even if your thoughts don't flow on a particular day, try to write a little bit, just to keep in stride.

3. Pick and Choose

A third suggestion is that you select the kind of notebook that will be best for you. You may prefer a spiral, a loose-leaf binder, or a book bound with blank pages. Decide whether you want to carry the notebook with you wherever you go or keep it in a private place. Whether you are going to carry your journal or leave it in one place has a lot to say about the kind of journal book you will use. Remember to choose a journal book that you will find easy to read years from now when you want to review your journal. Reviewing your journal is important in seeing how you grow. Reviewing gives you time to look at yourself and feel good about you today.

You might also want to choose a pen that you especially like. Sometimes a particular pen can make you feel like writing.

4. Give Yourself a Break

To use your journal, you must begin with an attitude of willingness. It is important to want to be willing to share yourself with yourself. *There are some prayers suggested in the back of the book that can be useful.* The Serenity Prayer is often helpful because it can be easily memorized. I use it, not only as an opening prayer to get my head and spirit together, but as a tool to keep my mind and spirit at ease as I write. It especially helps when I am distracted, when my mind wanders, or when I am anxious and just want to run away from writing. However you achieve it (prayer, yoga, drinking a glass of water, even a brief period of silence before you write), you will write best when you are most at ease. It is important to take some time to relax both your body and your mind before entering the world of your journal. Journal keeping may be one of the more important things you do. Take a good amount of time and give the journal your total attention. Forget the TV, forget the fight you had with your brother or sister, forget the bad exam, and forget the fear of not doing things right. There is no one right way. The right way for you is the way that helps you grow. So give yourself the kind of space you need to be comfortable enough to be honest with yourself.

5. Keep It to Yourself

A fifth rule is to try to keep your journal to yourself. If it is to be most useful to you, no one but you should ever see your journal. This is absolutely necessary to know. Don't fool yourself by saying that someday you'll show it to your teacher, mother, father, or special friend. If you write as if you are going to share your journal with anyone (even your closest friend), you are not likely to tell it as you see it. When you think about someone reading or hearing what you write, you are not likely to write exactly what you feel. You might begin to judge yourself, and judging yourself is what you want to avoid. Your journal is a book about you. It is your story. It tells about your special relationship with yourself and God as you find God in your life. It is a trust you set up with yourself. It can become kind of a personal "bible." Your journal can be a way in which you get to know yourself and discover God's will for you today. You have to insist to yourself that no one else will ever see what you have written. You might want to add the following contract to page 1 of your journal:

Because my journal is for me, I will keep it for my eyes only. By keeping it to myself, I know I can be honest.

6. Forget the Rules

A final suggestion is to forget about rules. There are no writing rules or grammar rules for journal keeping. Do not worry about spelling, grammar, or punctuation. Write however you can to express what you want to say. Write what you are thinking and feeling. Don't hold back any words, ideas, or feel-

16

ings. Write what you think, feel, and believe right now. Don't worry about what you once thought, believed, or felt. Don't worry about what you might think, believe, or feel some other day. Write clearly so that you will be able to read what you've written when you review your journal. There are no right or wrong ways to say what you think, feel, or believe, just as in your journal there are no right or wrong ways to think, feel, or believe. Don't cheat yourself. This journal is a gift to yourself.

Remember that there is a difference between talking and writing in your journal. When you talk with someone you want that person to understand what you are saying and what you mean. When you write in your journal you are trying to understand yourself and your world. Understanding yourself in new ways may not come to you right away, but it will come. You can learn about yourself through your journal if you write only for yourself.

7. Review, Review

Your goal will be to go beyond today. You will want to review your journal regularly. When you review it, you may be surprised. Things that might have been important to you a week, month, or year ago may have little importance to you today. Things you thought unimportant a while ago may be very important to you today. Beyond that, you will begin to see patterns in your life. You will ask yourself what things keep happening. Which do not? How have you changed in handling similar situations? What ways have you not changed? What ways would

17

you wish to change? What choices and decisions made in the past bring you the most comfort and peace today?

The Rest of the Book

In the very next chapter, you will begin your journal with exercises on how to find yourself *today*. There will be questions and exercises to help you see yourself as you think, feel, and believe today. You will write about what you do well and not so well. You will describe when you feel good and not so good.

Then we will suggest ways to look at yesterday and the yesterdays before that. You will write about things that have happened to you and how they made you feel. You will have a chance to think about those things once more and to ask yourself what these things mean to you today. Then, you can look at what you might want to do in the future. You will describe some goals and what you think you will do to make them happen.

We want to share with you the tools that will help make your journal more useful. Writing about important parts of your dreams might give you a whole new way of looking at yourself. Discovering how to describe your feelings will also be useful to you.

One of the most exciting parts of journal keeping is imaginary conversation. In an imaginary conversation in your journal, you can say things to people you might not be able to say face-to-face. In imaginary conversations you can even talk to people you don't know. Imaginary conversations let you talk with friends, enemies, relatives, people from history, even people you invent in your imagination. You will be able to be anywhere, any time in the past or the future, with anyone. The list of possibilities is long and exciting.

We will also try to show you how to review what you have recorded in your journal. When you review, you will be able to see what is important to you. When you go back and read what you have written, you will have the chance to rediscover your thoughts, feelings, and beliefs. Reviewing your journal can change you in some way and help you to be comfortable with that change.

All through the book there will be reminders that your journal is your gift to yourself. Your journal can help you see yourself better. Your journal can help you be at ease with whom you see.

Good luck. And remember—God is with you. You will find this to be true often in the pages of the journal you are beginning.

Chapter 2

Just for Today

Ask yourself: Who am I today? Who do I think I am right now?

Like most simple questions, these are not as simple as they look, and there are a number of ways to answer them. We have already discussed the roles and masks that others see when they are with you. There are a number of ways in which you can describe yourself. There are at least as many ways for others to describe you. You can think of yourself as Oriental, black, Caucasian, Indian, or Hispanic. You can see yourself as a young woman or a young man. You can be a citizen of the United States, Canada, Australia, Vietnam, Puerto Rico, or anywhere. You can see yourself as jogger, student, worker, baseball star, or anything else you do. If you are a woman and not a man, if you are black and not Oriental or Caucasian, if you play baseball rather than watch it, all of these say something about you. These things also say something about how others look and will look at you.

A well-known teacher used to say that he was among the lowest human beings in the world. He described himself as white (Caucasian), male, American, and Christian. He said that, to a major part of the world's population, he was the enemy. The people to whom he referred were people who had been hurt by white male Americans. As a white or Caucasian, he was part of a group that often treated people badly just because they were yellow, black, brown, or red—just because they were different. As a man, he knew he was part of the group of persons who throughout history were often responsible for keeping women from getting an equal chance at life. As an American (from the United States), the teacher said that he was a citizen of a nation that, although it had done much for world unity and peace, was also blamed for certain bad dealings with other countries—including participation in wars. Finally, this teacher said that as a Christian, because of the ways in which some Christians had chosen not to follow their beliefs, and because of the sad history of Christian prejudice against Jews, he was again part of a group that others considered dishonest and bad. This does not mean that the teacher himself was bad or dishonest, or that he chose to hurt others. It does mean that someone who did not know him could see him this way because of some of the masks he wore simply by circumstance.

As it was, he was quite happy. He saw himself as a generous person who loved and shared his learning through his life. He knew that he was a man of strong belief. Though he knew he often fell short of perfectly believing, he was at peace because he was trying to know himself and the God he found in his world.

In journal keeping, you should try not to let your particular masks and roles close your mind. Try to see as many ways as possible to get to know yourself and others. Look deeply and keep looking. Be open to new information and new feelings. Be ready to get rid of old ideas and feelings when they do not help you live at ease with yourself today. Try not to come to any quick decisions about yourself or anyone else or anything.

Because this man could see himself as being at ease with himself and his God, he was also able to feel comfortable looking at himself as a white male American Christian. He knew that white male American Christians have made important contributions to world unity and peace on spiritual, financial, political, racial, educational, and many other levels.

He knew that the Christian culture of which he was a part has done a lot to help people be more able to care and share. He knew that Christians have carried a belief that has asked people to love themselves and love one another.

As an American, he knew that his nation has emphasized peace among its people and the people of the world; that equal rights and concern for one another are part of the principles and the action of the United States. He believed in many of the values of the American Constitution and way of life.

As a man, he knew that he could and did respect woman. He knew many other men who had openly worked toward helping create a world where people could become more themselves and at peace with one another.

He was a man who had come to know and love himself. We wish the same for you.

You journal can be one of the most useful and rewarding ways of arriving at the self-knowledge and self-love that you seek. The first exercises will be concerned with how you see yourself and how others see you. Bit by bit, as honestly as you can, you will be drawing a portrait of yourself. It will be a first important step on the road you will be traveling the rest of your life.

Before you write anything, before you begin your first exercise, look at the suggested plan for each writing session. Read the plan and think about it for a moment before you move on. And for a while, until you have your own plan, you will find it helpful to refer back to it before beginning to write.

24

A Plan for
Each Exercise

The simple plan we suggest is as follows:

1. Get yourself comfortable in your private place.
2. Make sure you have your book, journal note-book, a pen or pencil.
3. Open with a prayer or thought that reminds you that you are doing something for yourself and with your God (for example, the Serenity Prayer, or one of those in chapter 7).
4. Read what you wrote during your last session.
5. Complete the following statements, writing about three or four sentences for each:

   When I look at what I wrote, I am most pleased about _____.
   I would most like to change _____.
   I'm really glad that I wrote about _____.
   I forgot to write _____.

6. This is a good time to thank yourself and your God for helping you share yourself in your journal. A simple "thank you for letting me be me" is a reminder of this special gift you give yourself which you call your journal.
7. Don't forget that each exercise is designed to help you get to know yourself and your world. Be as honest as you can today. Remember there are no perfect answers. There is only one perfect way to keep a journal, and that is honestly.
8. Now you are ready to write.

Exercise One

- Before you do anything else, read through the simple plan on page 25.
- Choose some moment in your life that you might feel comfortable writing about. The best day to write about is probably today. But if you prefer, you can choose some other moment.
- Record in your journal the time, date, and place that you will be writing about. If other people were with you at the time, write down their names too.
- Now answer the following questions in your journal as honestly and as thoughtfully as you can. But remember, it is more important to record the information than to understand it right away.
- This part of the journal may take you several days, even weeks. That's okay. Speed is not important. Being honest and answering every question is what will help you the most. A famous writer was once asked for advice on how to begin writing a big work, such as a novel. He answered in a way that can help us keep on the track in writing a journal. It may help you. He said, "First you write one sentence that is true. Then you write another."

True sentences are not easy to write. But you can do it. You don't need to write perfect sentences or perfect stories. You need to write your story. You need to write it in a way that will help you. Just write whatever comes into your head. Your journal, like your life, will become fuller and closer to you in time.

Now here are some questions to help you begin.

1. *Age.* I am _____ years old.
2. *Young woman or young man.* I am a young ____.
3. *Red, yellow, brown, black, white.* I am _____.
4. *Location in your family.* How many children are there? In which order were you born? I am the _____ (number) of ____ children.
5. *Parents.* I live with both my parents. I live with only my _____ (mother, father). My parents are divorced. My _____ (father, mother, parents) is/are dead. I do not live with my parents. I live with _____.
6. My *national background* is _____ (French, Pakistani, American, etc.).
7. *Money.* I think of myself as having _____ (no, a little, a lot, etc.) money.
8. *Geography.* I live in the _____ (North, East, South, West, Midwest, etc.) part of this country.
9. *Health.* I think I am _____ (healthy, not so healthy, sick).
10. *Knowledge.** I know a lot about _____.
    *List as many things that you know that are important to you. Include sports, learning from books and school, and things you have learned on your own.
11. *Skills.** I am able to _____.

27

*List all the things you have worked at to be able to do well. Include hobbies, jobs, things you've had special training in such as music or art, and things you have learned on your own.

12. *Appearance.* I look _____ . I am _____ .
*List your weight, height, eye color, hair color, skin color, and anything else you think of when you think about how you look.

13. *Limitations.* I am unable to _____ . I am most able to _____ . I am really good at _____ . I'm not so good at _____ .
*List the things you believe you cannot do well or are totally unable to do today. List the things you can do best today.

14. *Liking me.* I especially like myself because (when) _____ .
What I really like about myself is _____ .

15. *Disliking me.* I especially dislike myself because (when) _____
What I really dislike about myself is _____ .

16. *Success.* I feel successful when _____ .
I am most likely to succeed at _____ .
Success is important to me when _____ .

17. *Failure.* I feel a failure when _____ .
I am most likely to fail at _____ .
Failure is important to me when _____ .

18. I am most *proud* of _____ .

19. I am most *ashamed* of _____ .

20. Choose a *name* for yourself. Use one word you think best describes you.

21. If you could be another species (animal, bird, insect, fish, flower, reptile, etc.), what would you

be? Which animal would you most like to be?

22. If you could paint a picture that would tell you what you think about yourself, what things would be in the picture? What colors would you use? What one image or object in your picture would tell you most about how you see yourself?

23. When you *dream,* do you dream some of the same dreams over and over? Describe one of your favorite dreams. Then describe a dream that is your least favorite.

24. *Joy.* I am most joyful when _____.

25. *Sadness.* I am most sad when _____.

26. *Fear.* I am most afraid when _____. I am afraid of _____.

27. *Likes.* I like _____.

28. *Dislikes.* I dislike _____.

29. *In the Future.* In the future I would like to be _____. In the future I would like to try _____.

30. *Fantasies.* If anything in the world were possible, I would _____.

Exercise Two

- Before you do anything else, go back and read the simple plan on page 25. Follow its suggestions for beginning a new exercise.

Now you are ready for the next stage of your journal. Again, you will be finding out more things about yourself. In some ways, this exercise digs a bit deeper. These new questions and statements deal with how you see yourself when you are with other people. The questions deal with such topics as older people in your life, people your own age, people who can tell you what to do, people who like you, people who dislike you—in general, how people affect you and how they affect the way you see yourself. This exercise is divided into sections, so you can break up your journal-keeping times into as many time periods as you want. But we do suggest that each time you begin to write you follow the simple plan on page 25.

And don't forget—you needn't worry about perfect spelling or grammar. Just write clearly enough so that you will be able to read it again.

Now you can begin to write.

HAPPINESS. *Am I a happy person?*

I am happy when _____.
I would be happy if _____.
For me, happiness is _____.
I am unhappy when _____.
I would be unhappy if _____.
For me, unhappiness is _____.

BEING LIKE EVERYONE ELSE. *Do I want to be like everyone else?*

I feel different when _____.
I need to feel part of the crowd when _____.
I need to "fit in" because _____.
I like to be an individual when _____.
Feeling different is _____.
I wish I could be like _____.

STUBBORNNESS. *Do I like things always my way?*

When people don't do things the way I like, I feel _____.
When I know I am right, I _____.
Even when I know I am wrong, I sometimes _____.
After trying hard and knowing I cannot finish something, I _____.
If people would do things my way, _____.
I find it hard to tell the truth when _____.

JUDGING OTHERS. *Do I judge others even without all the facts?*

People who are rich are _____.

People who are poor are _____.

A person's color can tell me _____.

A person's age can tell me _____.

People who do well in school _____.

People who do well in sports _____.

All women _____.

All men _____.

CREATIVITY. *Am I creative?*

I think creative people are _____.

I am creative when _____.

To be creative means that I _____.

The most creative person I know _____.

The most creative person in history _____.

The best thing anybody has ever made _____.

CITIZENSHIP. *Am I a good citizen?*

To me, being a good citizen means _____.

I am a good citizen when _____.

To a good citizen, people from other countries are _____.

Being a good citizen is more than _____.

Just because I live in this country _____.

We suggest you end the exercise here. If you choose to stop writing, do so. When you begin the next exercise, see the instructions for exercise one on page 26. You may wish to close with a prayer of thanks. However, if you choose to continue, turn the page for the next exercise.

Exercise Three

- Before you do anything else, review the simple plan on page 25. Follow its suggestions for beginning a new exercise.

STUDENT and WORKER. *Am I a good student? Am I a good worker?*

To me, a good student is _____.
To me, a good student does _____.
I am a good student when _____.
I study when _____.
I work well when _____.
To me, hard work is _____.
When I work, I want _____.

SEXUALITY. *What do I think about my own sexuality?*

To me, my body is _____.
Sex is more than _____.
What frightens me most about sex is _____.
What I don't understand about sex is _____.
What I like most about my sexuality is _____.
What I learned from others about sex is _____.

NOT CARING. *What things and people don't I care about?*

I don't care about people who _____.
I don't care if _____.
I don't care about my life when _____.
I do not even want to read about _____.
Since people don't care about _____.
I'm "turned off" by _____.

AUTHORITY. *Do I respect authority?*

People in authority, like parents and teachers, _____.
People in authority get in my way when _____.
People in authority help me when _____.
I do not like the fact that people in authority _____.
I am glad that people in authority _____.
The person in authority I most like is _____.
The person in authority I least like is _____.
If I could be a person in authority, I would _____.

HONESTY. *Am I honest?*

I fear being honest with _____.
I fear being honest about _____.
I am most honest with _____.
I am most honest about _____.
I would like to be honest _____.
I am honest _____.
To me, honesty is _____.
To me, dishonesty is _____.

MATURITY. *Am I mature?*

I feel mature when _____.
To me, maturity is _____.
The most mature person I know _____.
A mature person is _____.
A mature person does _____.
I am more mature today _____.
Mature is a word that _____.
Some people think that a mature person _____.
To my mother, a mature person is _____.
To my father, a mature person is _____.
To my teacher, a mature person is _____.

We suggest that you end the exercise here. If you choose to stop writing, do so. When you begin the next exercise, see the instructions for exercise one on page 26. You may wish to close with a prayer of thanks. If you choose to continue, turn the page for another exercise.

Exercise Four

● Before you begin, review the simple plan on page
25. Follow its suggestions for beginning a new
exercise.

PLAY. *Do I know how to play?*
When I play, _____ .
The way I play that makes me feel best is
_____ .
I used to play _____ .
If I could play anything at all, I would play
_____ .
I like to play with _____ .
I never want to stop playing _____ .
Playing makes me feel _____ .

DEATH. *What do I think about death?*
When I think of death, _____ .
One thing about death that frightens me _____ .
Death can be happy _____ .
Someone special to me who died _____ .
Something about death I really don't understand
is _____ .
One thing about death that doesn't bother me is
_____ .
When I die, _____ .
When someone I know dies, _____ .

LIKING YOURSELF. *Do I like myself?*

What I like most about myself is _____.
I feel good about being me when _____.
All I have to do to make myself happy is _____.
I usually like myself when _____.
I usually do not like myself when _____.
The best thing about me is _____.

BEING A FRIEND. *Am I a good friend?*

I am a good friend to _____.
I am a good friend when _____.
To me, a good friend is _____.
To me, a good friend does _____.
I always have time for _____.
When I am angry with my friends, I _____.
When I am happy with my friends, I _____.

MY FRIENDS. *Who are my friends?*

My real friends are _____.
My friends always _____.
My special friend is _____.
My special friend does _____.
This person is my special friend because _____.
What I like most about my friends is _____.
What I like most about my special friend is _____.
When I feel hurt, my friends _____.

CARING FOR OTHERS. *Do I care for others?*

When I see someone hurting, I _____.

When I see a friend hurting, I _____.

When I see a person who looks afraid, I _____.

When my friend looks afraid, I _____.

People who need my help are _____.

People who just need to know I care are _____.

I show that I care by _____.

I show that I care when _____.

We suggest you end the exercise here. If you choose to stop writing, do so. When you begin the next exercise, see the instructions on page 26. You may wish to close with a prayer of thanks. If you choose to continue, turn the page for another exercise.

Exercise Five

● Review the plan on page 25 and use its suggestions for starting a new exercise.

ACTION. *How do I act?*
When I am in a jam, I _____.
If telling the truth is going to hurt, I _____.
If I want something, I just _____.
When I see something I want _____.
If something is bothering me, _____.
When I have to wait, _____.
Planning is _____.

SEEING MYSELF. *How do I see myself?*
When I am with people, _____.
When I am alone, _____.
Being by myself is _____.
Being with others is _____.
Sharing with others is _____.
If I had to be alone forever, _____.
When I have a problem, other people _____.
When I have a problem, I usually _____.

SATISFACTION. *Am I satisfied with myself?*

Compared to me, everyone _____.

If people knew who I really was _____.

When I'm trying hard and make a mistake, ____.

When I have to do something new, _____.

When I have to do something difficult, _____.

When I'm right and someone yells at me, _____.

When I'm wrong and someone yells at me, ____.

I know I deserve _____.

I don't deserve _____.

FAMILY. *Do I share with my family?*

My family gives me _____.

To me, a family should _____.

To me, a family should not _____.

The most important thing I can give my family ___.

The hardest thing for me to share with my
family _____.

I enjoy my family _____.

I don't enjoy my family _____.

I make my family better when _____.

I give my family _____.

41

SHYNESS. *When am I shy?*

When I don't want anyone to know I'm shy, ___.
It's very hard to cover up being shy when ___.
I think I am shy when ___.
I'm glad that I am not shy when ___.
To me, shyness is ___.
Shy people are ___.
I don't need to be shy ___.

INTERESTS. *What am I interested in?*

I spend most of my time ___.
When I have nothing to do, ___.
Music is ___.
Art is ___.
Books are ___.
Exercise is ___.
I most enjoy ___.
I least enjoy ___.
If I could do anything, I'd ___.

We suggest that you end the exercise here. If you choose to stop writing, do so. When you begin the next exercise, see the instructions for exercise one on page 26. You may wish to close with a prayer of thanks. If you choose to continue, turn the page for another exercise.

Exercise Six

- Reread the simple plan on page 25 for starting a new exercise and follow its suggestions. By now, of course, you may have your own plan. Use it if it makes you more comfortable and the writing exercises as profitable.

SHARING. *Do I have time for others?*
I share with others _____.
I especially like sharing _____.
I prefer not to share _____.
When I share I _____.
When I don't share, I _____.
To me, sharing is _____.
To me, sharing is not _____.

SELF-CONTROL. *Do I have self-control?*
To me, self-control is _____.
To me, self-control is not _____.
Self-control helps _____.
When I'm very angry, I _____.
When I'm very happy, I _____.
When I'm scared or confused, I _____.

HUMOR. *When do I have a sense of humor?*

Someone who has a sense of humor is _____.

Someone who has a sense of humor does _____.

To me, having a sense of humor is more than __.

It's hard to have a sense of humor when _____.

It's hard to have a sense of humor about _____.

Having a sense of humor can help _____.

I need to be able to laugh at myself _____.

MONEY. *How do I take care of money?*

To me, money is _____.

I never have enough money _____.

When I want something for which I do not have the money, _____.

Even when I have enough money, I sometimes __.

To get money, I _____.

I borrow money _____.

I like money when _____.

I don't like money when _____.

I lend money _____.

I give money _____.

UNIQUENESS. *What do I see as special about me?*

I am especially good at _____.

What I like most about me is _____.

When I am with others, they enjoy the way I ___.

I enjoy being different _____.

Being different helps me _____.

Everybody is the same in _____.

Everybody is different in _____.

The one thing I want people to remember about me _____.

Now you have completed six exercises. During the exercises, you have been putting together in your journal a rough picture of how you see yourself to-day. There was no right way to do these exercises. There was no correct way to answer. You wrote what you believed to be true about yourself. You did the best you could. Remember your journal is for you. In the beginning of this book we suggested that you never share your journal with anyone. We explained that in order to be totally honest, you had to write only for you. But sometimes these exercises you write bring up questions or problems you think you might need to share with someone. That's good. One way your journal can help you to grow is by helping you figure out the things that trouble, confuse, frighten, or please you about yourself or your world.

45

If you discover that you need to share something, write it down on a separate piece of paper. You might wish to thank God for helping you see it. You might ask God's guidance in selecting someone you can trust to help you understand yourself better. Using the Serenity Prayer can help us to "accept the things we cannot change" and to "change the things we can" change, and it also gives us a chance "to know the difference."

Something that helps me is my "God bag." I keep a brown paper bag in my room. On the outside of the bag, I write *God bag.* When I am writing or reviewing my journal, I keep a small pad next to me. On that pad I write the things I find in my journal that trouble, confuse, or frighten me. At the end of a writing session, I fold the paper and put it in my God bag. Once a month, I read all the notes. If something no longer troubles, confuses, or frightens me, I write it in my journal. I usually just begin by saying, "These things used to confuse, trouble, or frighten me, but they don't anymore." Then I thank my God for helping me change the things I can change. For the things that still trouble, confuse, or frighten me, I ask for God's help. There are some things that I know I need to share with someone I can trust. Sometimes that person is a teacher, a pastor, an older friend, or someone my own age. The important thing is that I must feel I can trust that person with what is hurting me.

I change what I can. At least I work at it. But there are some things I have to learn to accept and live with. I put those back in my God bag.

Right now, and at the end of any session with your journal, sit for a moment and relax. If you wish to, thank God for the guidance you have been given. Enjoy the things you have learned about yourself. Then close your journal, knowing that what you have learned may not help right away, knowing that it will take time to accept things and to change things, and knowing that you have done your best for today.

Chapter 3

Before Now

When a shopkeeper checks to see what he has to sell and what he needs to order, we say he is taking inventory. One object of inventory taking is to get rid of damaged or unsold goods. So the shopkeeper looks at the records of the things sold and then decides whether they are worth having in the store again or whether there are other things that would sell better. So far, in your journal, you have been doing what the shopkeeper might call inventory. You've been looking at yourself to see who you are and who you are not. You've had a chance to see things about yourself you like and things you don't like. You've begun to see where you are today, where you've come from, and things you'd like to change. During the exercises given in this chapter, try to look at what has happened in your life to make you who you are today.

You will be looking at events in your life that may have influenced what you do and how you see yourself today. As you look, you may find some surprises.

Now please open your journal. Briefly and quickly answer the question below. As you look for an answer, think back to your early childhood, preschool, elementary school.

Here is the question. Write your answer in your journal.

What are the five most important things that have happened in your life?

These five things will be the basis for your journal keeping for at least the next five exercises. In these exercises, you will be examining what happened. Who did what to whom; when; where; how? What happened to you as a result? How have people, places, and things affected you?

Exercise One

- To begin this important exercise in your journey toward better knowing yourself and your world, try to do the following:

1. Reread the suggested plan for a good journal session on page 25 and follow its suggestions.
2. Open your journal to the page on which you answered the question on page 50.
3. Try to get yourself together and with your God. Instead of a lot of words or a regular prayer, you may wish to be silent for a minute, or slowly repeat for a minute one of the brief prayers in chapter 7.
4. Read your five answers.
5. Choose one of them to write about in this exercise.
6. In your journal briefly answer the following questions about what happened:
   > What happened?
   > What happened to you?
   > How old were you?
   > Who else was there?
   > What "made it happen"?
   > Where did it happen?
   > Why do you think it happened?
7. Now spend about ten or fifteen minutes writing the story in your journal. Tell the story as you believe it happened. You can be honest because you are telling your story only to yourself. The

only correct way to tell your story is your way.

8. Now read the story you wrote in number 7 above.

9. Answer the following questions about your story.

How did what happened make you feel?

Would you like it to happen again?

List how each person in the story felt. List each person by name.

How did you know how each one felt? Explain by name.

How did each person show how she or he felt? Explain by name.

How did you show how you felt?

How do you feel about it now?

Did you ever dream about what happened?

What happened in your dream?

Did you like the dream?

How do you feel now when you read your story?

10. Choose something that happened either in your story or while writing in your journal today for which you are thankful. Take time now to thank your God for helping you to be able to be thankful. You may wish to simply say, "Thank you, God, for letting me be me," or another prayer. Remember, if you cannot think of anything else to be thankful for, you can be thankful for having a journal and for being able to write in it.

Exercise Two

When you being to think about an event from your life, it is often easier to recall what has happened to you *because* of the event. In the last exercise, we tried to give you some questions that would help you dig behind what you felt happened to get to some of the facts and even the ways other people saw and felt the same experience. No experience that you remember can be unimportant. A fight, a stolen bicycle, the death of a grandparent, an automobile accident, being called a "sissy," losing a game, moving, changing schools, getting a new dog, getting a bad or a good mark—all are important. Remember when you write this exercise that you are interested in finding out about you and how you feel. Remember that when you think about other people and how they feel, you can better understand yourself. Trying to understand how people, places, and things affect you is a long process. Just let go and write what you think.

1. Get yourself comfortable in your private place.
2. Make sure you have your book, journal notebook, a pen or pencil.
3. Open with a prayer or thought that reminds you that today is a gift to you (for example, the Lord's Prayer, or the Prayer of Saint Francis as found in the last chapter).
4. Read what you wrote during your last session.
5. Now complete the following statements, writing about three or four sentences for each:

When I look at what I wrote, I am most pleased about _____.
I'm glad I looked at _____.
I think I've learned more about _____.
I'd like to learn more about _____.

6. This is a good time to thank yourself and your God for helping you share yourself in your journal. It is also a time when you could ask your God to help you to be willing to be honest. Sometimes it helps just to say, "Help me be the me that you know I can be." Or, the phrase adapted from the Lord's Prayer, "thy will, not mine, be done."

7. Open your journal to the page on which you answered the question on page 50.

8. Read the four remaining answers you wrote to the question on page 50.

9. From the four remaining events, select one that had more people than you in it. If one of the experiences was unpleasant for you, that would be a good one to choose for this exercise.

10. Write in your journal the experience you have chosen.

11. Answer the following questions about your story:

    How did what happened make you feel?
    Could it happen again?
    Why could it happen again?

List what each person did. List each person by name. (For example: William hit the dog.) List how each person's actions made you feel. List each person by name (For example: William made me feel bad because _____ .)

> How did each person feel about what happened? How did you know how each person felt?

12. Now spend fifteen or twenty minutes telling the story of what happened. As you write in your journal, tell the story as you believe it happened. You can be honest because this story is your story. Only you know this story.

13. Before you answer number 14, read your story.

14. The following questions can help you better understand yourself and your story. Answer them in your journal. Write as much as you want. You don't have to answer every question, but each one is here to help you.

> Who were you at the time of the story?
>
> How does what happened make you feel about yourself?
>
> Who in the story is most like you?
>
> If you could be anyone else in the story, who would you be?
>
> If you could change anything in this story, what would you change?

15. Choose something that happened either in your story or today about which you are afraid. Ask your God to help you to be willing to have the fear taken away. When I am afraid, I often pray the Twenty-third Psalm or the Serenity Prayer. If you have your own special prayer, use that. Some people simply say, "Lord, I'm afraid. Help me." This may be a good time to use your God bag.

Exercise Three

Everyone goes through pleasant and unpleasant experiences. Somehow, many of us think that no one else can understand what we experience—that no one else has gone through the same thing. Really, no one does go through things the way you do. Most people, however, are affected by much the same things. Each of us shows the way we are affected in our own way. Some people laugh when afraid. Some people look scared. Some people chatter. Some people smile. Some even act brave. Everybody has ways to deal with pleasant and unpleasant experiences. Writing about being afraid can make what you fear have less power over you. It might even make the fear disappear. This exercise is designed to help you see things from another point of view. Although it may help you understand others, its purpose is to give you a way to help you understand your own feelings about things that happen and about being yourself. It's so easy to feel "different" or "unique." If you see only the ways in which you are different, you could end up lonely and afraid.

Throughout this exercise, try to see your experience through another's eyes.

1. Get yourself comfortable in your private place.
2. Make sure you have your book, journal notebook, a pen or pencil.
3. Open with a prayer or thought that helps you feel less alone, less afraid. Some people like to use the first part of the Hail Mary, the angel's

56

greeting to Mary: "Hail Mary, full of grace, the Lord is with you." You might remember that these words were said to Mary at a very scary time in her life, a time when she felt she was being asked by God to do some extraordinary things. Of course, any prayer or thought that helps you feel comfortable will be just fine.

4. Slowly and carefully, read the story you wrote during the last exercise.

5. Ask yourself as you read, "How does this make me more me today?"

6. Now you are ready to write. This time you are going to tell the same story again, but it may not look like the same story. Choose one of the other persons in the story. Name the person. In your journal answer the following questions:

> What would that person see?
>
> What would that person feel?
>
> How would others know what that person felt?
>
> What did that person do?
>
> What happened to that person?
>
> How did what happened make that person feel about herself or himself?
>
> What did the person do that was different from what you did? Why?
>
> How did the person feel that was different from how you felt? Why?

7. Now rewrite the story as the other person would have seen, felt, and acted. We suggest you write for fifteen to twenty minutes.

8. Look at this story again. Answer the following questions as if you were going to rewrite the ending of the story.

How could you make the story end in a way that would be pleasant for everybody in the story?

What did you change to make it pleasant?

Or, if the story had such an ending:

Why did you see this ending as pleasant for everybody?

What happened to make it pleasant?

9. Close with a simple act of trust in God's goodness. For example, "Lord, I know you are not going to make anything happen to me today that you and I cannot handle together."

Exercise Four

Clues to the past are often found in old letters, postcards, and notes sent to people. Sometimes being away from people you care about and who you feel care about you gives you the distance to share feelings and experiences you might otherwise keep to yourself. Reading a letter you wrote to someone who cares can be another way to get to know yourself. In this session you will write such a letter.

1. Get yourself comfortable in your private place.
2. Make sure you have your book, journal notebook, a pen or pencil.
3. For an opening prayer, take a minute to think about what Jesus meant when he asked you to "love your neighbor as yourself."
4. In this exercise we do not suggest you review your last exercise. Exercise three had its own review in it. In some ways, exercise three was a review of exercise two.
5. Read the three remaining answers you wrote to the question on page 50.
6. Select one of the three remaining events. Choose one that was very difficult for you to understand, or one that you have been unable to share. If none of the three are like that, choose one that you think could teach you most about yourself today.
7. Write the experience from your original list on the first page for exercise four in your journal.
8. Think about the people in your life. Choose one

59

person you believe you can really trust. If you don't know someone you can trust with this experience, make up a person.

9. Spend at least the next fifteen to twenty minutes writing to that person. Remember, you are the only person who will ever see the letter. The letter is a way to help you share with yourself. It can give you a chance to see what happened in a way you may have never seen before. You may say anything and everything you wish. Make sure you include everything. Answer the following questions:

Who did what to whom?
Why?
How?
What happened because of it?

Make sure you say exactly what you feel and how you feel. Don't forget this is a letter to someone who cares. It is not an essay that you will be graded on. Be as honest as you are able to be today.

10. Before you answer number 11, read your letter.
11. Writing as much or as little as you want, try to answer each of the following questions.

What is there in your letter that tells you the experience was pleasant or unpleasant?
What do you want the reader of the letter to do for you?
What things are in your letter to someone you trust that could not be in a letter to another person?

Is there anything you understand better because you have written this letter? Explain.

Have you learned anything new about yourself? Explain.

Do you think that what happened to you has ever happened to anyone else? Why?

Could you help another person understand if it happened to them? How?

12. Take some time to think about the story the Gospels tell about Mary and Martha. Remember how different the two women were? Martha seemed to be always working. She wanted to make her friends comfortable. She cooked. She cleaned. She tried to make sure her friends had everything they needed. Martha wanted her friends to know she loved them, and she wanted to share her life with them. Mary also wanted to make her friends comfortable. When her friends came to visit, she sat with them. Mary listened to their every word. She paid attention to what her friends said and what they felt. Mary wanted her friends to know she loved them, and she wanted to share her life with them. Jesus was a friend of both women. He knew both loved him. Think about Mary and Martha. You may wish to read the story in Luke's Gospel (chapter 10 verses 38–42). Remember how different each woman was. Recall how Jesus loved each of them as he loves you today.

Exercise Five

Sometimes something happens to you that may seem like a shock. One day things are one way, and a few minutes, days, or weeks later, you find that things aren't that way at all. At other times, things happen and you just don't know how they happened. In this exercise you are going to have a chance to see how decisions, feelings, ideas, and ways of looking at life affect you. You will look at something that happened to you and try to discover what helped you see what happened. You will take an experience from your life that you feel is important and you will tell what was going on before you had that experience.

1. Get yourself comfortable in your private place.
2. Make sure you have your book, journal notebook, a pen or pencil.
3. Read the following brief passage from Scripture:

> When I was hungry, you gave me not to eat. . . . but when, Lord, did I see you hungry?

Think about the following questions:
> Why do you think the person in the story is surprised?
> What question does the person ask Jesus?
> What do you think about Jesus' answer?

4. Read the answer you wrote to the questions at the end of the last exercise (exercise four).

5. Now complete the following statements, writing one or two sentences for each:

    I'm glad I wrote about _____.
    When I look at what I wrote, I am most pleased about _____.
    Writing can help me share _____.
    Sharing by writing helps me _____.
    I forgot to write _____.

6. Read the two remaining answers you wrote to the question on page 50.

7. Select one from the two remaining events. Whichever you choose is fine. You may save the other to use later when you come back to these exercises on your own.

8. Write the experience you have selected in the section of your journal for exercise five.

9. Describe as carefully and completely as you can the event you listed in number 8 above. Remember to tell who did what. To whom? How? Why? And what happened because of it? Spend about ten minutes writing. Of course, if you need more time, take it.

10. Now take time to read what you wrote. If you left anything out of your story, add it now.

11. The purpose of this exercise is to help you understand how things happen and how what happens makes you feel. Take your time answering the following questions about the event you listed in number 8 above. Answer as best you can. Explain how you feel or how you felt.

Five minutes before the event occurred, what I most remember _____.

I was doing _____.

I was with _____.

I felt _____.

I was thinking about _____.

I wish I was _____.

I could have been _____.

The day before the event occurred, I most remember _____.

I was doing _____.

I was with _____.

I felt _____.

I was thinking about _____.

I wish I was _____.

I could have been _____.

The day after the event occurred, what I most remember _____.

I was doing _____.

I was with _____.

I felt _____.

I was thinking about _____.

I wish I was _____.

I could have been _____.

12. Read what you wrote for number 11 above.

13. Now spend the next ten to fifteen minutes completing each of the following:

> I remember the people, places, things, and feelings that were part of what happened before because _____.
>
> Remembering what happened before ____.
>
> I remember the people, places, things, and feelings that happened to me the day after because _____.
>
> Remembering what happened after ____.
>
> Today, when I remember the people, places, things, and feelings that were part of what happened, I _____.

14. Robert Frost wrote a poem about coming to a fork in the road of life and choosing one road rather than the other. He felt his choice made all the difference in his life. As you have seen in these exercises, things continually happen to you. Some things you see as pleasant, some unpleasant. Some people take unpleasant experiences and use them or make them positive and helpful by learning something about themselves or their world. When written honestly, these exercises can make what happens to you help you be more you. There is a poster that says, "When life hands you lemons, make lemonade ..." Think of one experience you wrote about that may have seemed like a lemon when it happened. Ask your God to help you to make or learn something from it that will help you be more you.

Chapter 4
Talking It Out—
Dialogue

If you have followed the journal-keeping process suggested by the exercises in the last two chapters, you have begun to find out a great deal about yourself.

As you look closely at experiences from your life, you may begin to see things you never saw and hear things you never heard before. The next five exercises are designed to help you fine tune your vision and your hearing. The technique we are going to use is called *dialogue*. A dialogue usually means a sharing between two people. The sharing may be in the form of discussion, writing, or any other means by which two people communicate. The key to remember in dialogue is that each person has something to share with the other. Each person may give, and each may receive. To participate in a dialogue, you have to make a choice to hear and see not only what you want to give and receive, but what the other person is giving and what the person desires to receive.

In the dialogue in the exercises in this chapter we are going to imagine what other people said, felt, and how they acted in certain situations in the past as well as what could be said, felt, and done in the future.

Journal dialogue is much like prayer. There are times when it is prayer. Prayer is sharing. In prayer, we share ourselves with God. When we pray we are open to God. A praying person is one who is open to God's will. When we pray we can use words, we can be silent, we can meditate on scenes from the Bible or nature, we can sing, we can paint—we can do whatever makes us open to God. A man who was called the Juggler of Our Lady even used his circus talents as a means of prayerful communication with God and God's family.

Writing can be a method of prayer as well as a way to be more open to yourself and others. Your intention and the effort you put behind it are far more important than whether you are a perfect writer or recorder of history.

Exercise One

1. Relax in that special private place.
2. Make sure you have your book, journal notebook, a pen or pencil.
3. Since these exercises are on dialogue, open this exercise by sitting in silence and listening to yourself breathe. After you have blocked out almost all else but your breathing, try repeating aloud or to yourself, in harmony with your breathing pattern, the following phrase adapted from the Lord's Prayer: "Your will not mine." This form of prayer is called *breath prayer* or *mantra*, and you find other forms of it in chapter 7.
4. Read the following journal entry by a high school student who came to her writing desk very angry with her brother.

Damn Ernie. He is always saying things to hurt me. Today he's up to his old tricks again. Damn. damn damn damn Damn DAMN. Who does he think he is? Just because I'm younger he somehow thinks he's superior. I just won't accept that.

He said the reason that I didn't make cheerleading squad was because I didn't try hard enough. He said I didn't practice my routines enough. He even told dad that I didn't want to be on the team. How can that be true—it's one of the main ways to be popular in school. It could be a change for me to get better known. Damn Ernie.

Of course I want to be popular. But not like Sarah the squad captain. I wouldn't want to be popular like she is. She's such a phony the way she cuts up everyone behind their back. I think because she's captain and has power everyone's afraid of her. Even when she's nasty people just let her get away with it.

I wonder if all that power was what I wanted. Power and popularity. That had to be it because that's bull cheering others on and not playing yourself. I really don't think it helps the players much either. In fact I think it just makes those with big heads think more about themselves and less about the team.

Besides, I don't want to spend a semester running about with Sarah, pretending smiles, competing for popularity when I can use the fall to get my studies in shape and then try out for the basketball team. After all, I know I'm good, and even with homework I still find time to dunk a few baskets for almost an hour every day.

Maybe Ernie was right in a way. I guess I just couldn't say what I wanted. Well, any way, he didn't have to say it in that tone and run to dad without asking me what was up.

5. Here the journal writer went from being angry with her brother to openness about herself. Not

only did she gain a better understanding of her halfhearted attempt to make the cheerleading squad, she came to a better understanding of who she is and what she wants. In some of her later journal writing she has been more able to see how the pressure of trying to be popular can be turned aside while she gets on to finding out who she sees herself as being. She has seen that the desire for acceptance and approval often keeps her from pleasing others and herself. If she had shared her real feelings with her brother, he might have better understood. If she had not feared what her father wanted from her and what he would say, she might have found him accepting rather than disappointed.

6. Reread number 4 above.
7. After you have read number 4, answer the following questions, writing one or two sentences for each:

> What kind of person is the girl who wrote the journal?
>
> What in her journal tells you that?
>
> What kind of person is her brother?
>
> What in the journal tells you that?
>
> What kind of person is her father?
>
> What in the journal tells you that?

8. Now read what you wrote for number 7 above.
9. Even though the journal writer learned a lot about herself, it is very likely that you had some difficulty answering the questions in number 7 above, for the journal entry did not contain much dialogue with others. Now, rewrite your

version of the story. When you write your version, include the exact words that you think each person might have said. Try to put words in each person's mouth that would seem to fit according to the journal entry. Make sure you include the journal writer, her brother, and her father. Use such phrases as *she said, her father said,* and *her brother said* to introduce each part of the dialogue. Take at least twenty minutes to do this part of the exercise. You may wish to spend several writing sessions on the dialogue.

10. After writing the dialogue, close your journal.

11. Now take some quiet time to read the following reflection:

> On Listening
> by Jan Radlowski
>
> If I approach
> each person I meet,
> each problem I encounter,
> each step I take,
> in a relaxed frame of mind,
> what I need will come to me,
> and much more quickly than
> if I strain and hurry;
> for, relaxed, I hear and see
> what is, not
> what I think should or ought be.

12. Think about one time during the last day, week, or month when you were relaxed enough to hear or see something that helped you feel good about yourself. Take some time now to thank God for that opportunity.

Exercise Two

There are other aspects of dialogue besides words. Communicating with another person involves not only what is said by the speaker, but what is heard, seen, and felt by the listener. In this exercise you are going to explore more deeply the journal entry you read and wrote about in the last exercise.

1. Relax in that special private place.
2. Make sure you have your book, journal notebook, a pen or pencil.
3. The theme of the exercises in this chapter on dialogue is really "live and let live." Most of us need this reminder quite often. We need to realize that we are not equipped to judge or criticize others for what they are, do, say, or feel. Jesus called us to have a full life. His example offers hope to all of us, for he showed that God loves each of us as we are—even when we fail to love ourselves. From the cross, he begged, "Father, forgive them, for they know not what they do."

As a form of opening prayer, make a list of no more than five things you have said or done in the last twenty-four hours that have hurt you or others. Remember, your journal is for your eyes only. After each item on the list, write the phrase, "Father, forgive me. Let me live and let others live." This is called a *litany of forgiveness*.

Example: *"I told John how really dumb he looked. Father, forgive me. Let me live and let others live."*

You may wish to try doing this exercise on a regular basis (daily, weekly). After you finish your litany, relax and go on to the next step.

4. Take time to reread numbers 4 and 9 in the last exercise (page 69).

5. Now try to get beneath what is said in words so you can understand what is heard and felt by the people involved. You are going to choose five quotes from number 4 in the last exercise (page 69) and describe them in your journal by completing for each quote the phases that follow. But first, complete the example below.

> She said, (the quote) _____.
> When she said this, she felt _____.
> She felt this way because _____.
> The person talked about probably said __.
> Because he/she felt _____.
> In order to better understand, I would need to _____.

Here is the example to be completed:

> She said, <u>"Damn Ernie. He is always saying things to hurt me."</u>
> When she said this, she felt <u>angry and misunderstood.</u>
> She felt this way because _____.
> The person talked about probably said __.
> Because he/she felt _____.
> In order to better understand, I would need to _____.

6. Now choose five quotes from the journal entry in number 4 in the last exercise (page 69) and carefully describe them by completing for each the phrases listed in number 5 above. Make sure that

at least one quote you choose is near the beginning of the journal entry and one near the end. Spend about five minutes on each.

7. Now you are going to rewrite the dialogue using the phrases *she said, her brother said,* and *her father said.* This time, write it with a view to what she learned at the end of her journal entry. Try to help her to describe to herself, to her brother, and to her father what she really wants and how she really feels. In this rewrite, forget the anger, pain, and disappointment she started with and concentrate on what she discovered about herself. Write the dialogue from the point of view of "live and let live." Spend at least fifteen minutes on this.

8. Look over what you wrote for number 7 above. Ask yourself the following question: Is it always easy to know what I honestly need and want? In your journal, list five things that can get in the way when you try to get to know yourself. Then list five things that help you to get to know yourself.

9. As a closing prayer, read what you wrote in number 8 above. Ask God to remove those things that get in your way. Thank God for the things that help you get to know yourself. In thanksgiving, repeat softly aloud or to yourself the words of Jesus: "I have come that you might have life and have it to the fullest."

Exercise Three

So far you have looked at the journal entry in exercise one (page 69), in terms of the author, her brother, and her father. You have looked at the actual words she wrote and you have looked at some of the feelings behind the words. In numbers 5 and 6 (page 71) in the last exercise, you were encouraged to describe the kind of information you would need to better understand the situation in which the writer found herself. Now, you will have a chance to use those listening and seeing skills to create a dialogue.

1. Relax in that special private place.
2. Make sure you have your book, journal notebook, a pen or pencil.
3. The theme of this exercise on dialogue is "be yourself." Often, when we tend to judge or belittle others, it is because we feel so inadequate ourselves. At times, just for acceptance, we do what others want us to do or think we ought to do, even though we betray ourselves. On the other hand, just to be noticed, we can do the opposite of what others expect or desire. Trying to be anyone else, or trying to please others doesn't work. Often when we choose to do what we believe is right, others respect us, and those we respect stick close to us and offer us support.

Our dialogue with others says a lot about the shape of our dialogue with ourselves. How we share with God and others in our life is how we share with ourselves.

As a form of opening reflection, complete the following statements in your journal.

> I feel best about myself when _____.
> I am happiest about _____.
> I truly enjoy _____.
> I am most hopeful about _____.
> I know I can love myself when _____.
> Though it is difficult, I truly get a lot out of _____.
> For a long time, I have been working on _____.
> Nothing is as important to me as_____.
> I am most at ease when _____.
> Even when I am alone, I can _____.

After you have completed your answers, take a few minutes to quietly read them. Then thank God for helping you share with yourself by saying the Lord's prayer.

4. Being yourself is not easy. Look once more at number 4 in exercise one (page 69). This time concentrate on the writer's description of Sarah. Try to find out what you can about Sarah and the feelings the writer has about her.

5. After you have reread number 4 in exercise one, answer the following questions in your journal.

> Who is Sarah?
>
> What do you think she looks like?
>
> How old do you think she is?
>
> How do you think she deals with other people?
>
> How do you think she feels about herself?
>
> Do you think she has a lot of friends? Why?
>
> Does cheerleading take a lot of physical skill? How? What? Why?
>
> Does cheerleading take a lot of social skill? How? What? Why?
>
> How much of the writer's reaction to Sarah comes from her fear of being herself?
>
> Does the writer have more anger with herself or with Sarah?
>
> What would you need to know to better understand Sarah?

6. As you began to answer the questions in number 5 above, you probably came up with more questions. Really, it's hard to know who people are and what they mean. When you only have the writer's point of view and little experience with either person, it becomes even more difficult. If you were there, you might have understood better.

7. Go back and read your answers to the questions in number 5 above.
8. In the next twenty minutes, you are going to write four dialogues. Be precise, but write quickly. Do one after the other without stopping in between. Make sure you use the phrases *Sarah said, her friend said, the author of the journal said, the cheerleader said,* and so on. Have people say what you think they would. Write at least two pages of dialogue for each of the following conversations:

> Sarah and a girl friend
> Sarah and another girl wanting to be a cheerleader
> Sarah and a boyfriend
> Sarah and another cheerleader

Write quickly.
9. Without looking at your other journal entries, write a dialogue between the young woman who wrote the original journal entry in exercise one (page 69) and her father. In this dialogue, have her explain her feelings about her likes and dislikes. Have her clearly explain why she chooses not to be a cheerleader. Let her words tell you about her interest in basketball. Have her explain to her father who she feels she is today and how she feels about herself. Write at least two pages, but take as much time as you like. Make sure you let her father express his point of view.

10. Practicing dialogue with your journal is a chance to get close to yourself. Prayer is a form of dialogue. Sometimes dialogue can best be accomplished in silence, when we hear our own hopes, fears—our inner self. Silent prayer is a way to get close to yourself and God.

Close your journal. Spend a quiet minute or so considering how useful your journal is to you. Think about the gifts God gives you through it. Just sit there and be thankful for your journal that makes you more able to be you.

Close the exercise with the simple words, "Thank you, God, for helping me be me."

Exercise Four

Robert F. Kennedy once said, "Possibility must begin in dialogue. Dialogue is more than freedom to speak. It is the willingness to listen, and to act."

Taking action is risky. But once you make a choice and begin to act on it, you quickly discover that not every decision is forever. Because we are not perfect beings with infinite knowledge, it is possible to make what we think is the best possible decision and later find out that we are wrong. It is even possible to do what you believe is the right thing and find yourself unpopular with those from whom you wish approval or acceptance.

Perhaps more than words, feelings, or ideas, the most powerful form of dialogue we have with ourselves, with God, and with others is action. When we decide to act, we decide to participate in dialogue. In making a decision, we are sometimes unconsciously affected by the opinions, needs, and presence of other persons. Even when we make a decision for ourselves alone, in the long run it affects others. Even if no one knows what we have decided or done, we are changed by our every act, and in some way that change affects our dialogue with others. When we choose actions that help us feel good about ourselves, we eventually share that good feeling with others. Feeling good about yourself helps you know how to listen and be with others comfortably. It is when you are willing to be open to God and others that you can be most open to yourself.

1. Relax in that special place.
2. Make sure you have your book, journal notebook, a pen or pencil.
3. In preparation for this exercise about listening and acting, calmly read the following version of a section from Paul's letter to the people of Corinth.

> You are an open letter about Christ.
> Your letter is not written with pen and ink.
> Your letter is written in the Spirit of the living God.
> The message has been engraved, not in stone or gold, but in those with whom you share life.
>
> (adapted from 2 Corinthians 3:2–3)

Those with whom we choose to share, as well as those with whom we choose not to share, reflect the message of what we truly believe.

Describe briefly in your journal one situation in the last twenty-four hours in which you have chosen to share with another. Describe why you chose to share. Ask God to let the Spirit help you in your sharing. Ask to be able to listen more to God and to others. Thank God for enabling you to share. Slowly write the following phrase while saying it softly aloud or to yourself: "May your Word, O God, be known by my words."

4. So far in this chapter you have looked at someone else's life. Now you are going to look more closely at your own life. Think about a recent sit-

uation in your life in which, though you had the best intentions, you were not understood. If there's a situation in which you wished to do something good for another person or for yourself, take some time to think about what happened.

5. Using the situation you thought about in number 4 above, describe it in your journal by completing the following phrases in as much detail as you can.

What seemed to happen was _____.
What I wanted to happen was _____.
What seemed to go wrong was _____.
Though I had good intentions, _____.
The other person really did _____.
The other person really didn't _____.
I suppose I should have known _____.
If the situation were to happen again, ____.
The situation made me feel _____.
The situation made the other person(s) feel

_____.
The situation made me (do) _____.
The situation made the other person(s) (do)

_____.
I guess the choice was _____.
I really didn't see _____.
I guess I didn't know _____.
If I could do it over, _____.

Spend about twenty minutes on this segment.

6. Keeping in mind what you wrote in number 5 above, complete the following in your journal:

When I think about the situation, I feel good about _____.

When I think about the situation, I feel not so good about _____.

Spend about five minutes on this segment.

7. Read what you wrote in your journal in response to number 5 above. Complete the following in your journal:

If I could have said _____.

If I had known _____.

If I had heard _____.

I knew things weren't going well when the other person said _____.

Those words made me feel _____.

In response, I said _____.

Of course what I really wanted to say was

_____.

Because I felt like _____.

When I think about it, what I really wanted was _____.

What confused me most _____.

What I didn't know about the situation was

_____.

What I didn't know about myself was ____.

What I didn't know about the other person was _____.

Some things I knew but pushed out of my mind, such as _____.

The situation would have been better if I had only said _____.

The situation would have been better if I had only (done) _____.

When the whole thing was over, I felt ____.

Today, I feel _____.

Spend about twenty minutes on this segment.

8. In no more than five simple sentences describe the situation you thought about in number 4 above and wrote about in numbers 5, 6, and 7. Be brief.

9. As a closing reflection for this exercise, think about how often our words do not say what we wish to say—or what we feel. Think, too, of what wonderful tools words can be. Words express who we are and what we feel. Jesus is called "the Word." He is the Word of God made flesh—the living Word. Truly the message of Jesus is more than the words in the Bible or the words he spoke while alive centuries ago. He is "Word" because his message, though misunderstood and even rejected by man, is written in the spirit of men and women.

In a special way, we, too, are the word of God. For the only word of God that many people will ever hear is the life that we live. Our actions, too, speak to the hearts and spirits of men and women.

As a closing prayer, you may wish to use the following breath prayer or any other prayer from chapter 7.

Word of God, Word made flesh.

Exercise Five

When we share through words, other people often have a difficult time getting our message. Sometimes we're not sure of what we mean and what we feel. Even close friends who know who we are and what we believe can have a hard time. There are times when people either don't wish to hear our message or have already made up their minds. But more often than not, when we share important things, those who understand us understand not so much because of the words we choose, but because of who they know us to be. For people who know us, our words have a history. Those who know us best often know who our other friends are, what we believe, what we feel, and how we act in general. When we speak, our friends and those who know us "hear" all of those things, as well as the words we say.

Even then, no person ever understands us one hundred percent of the time.

1. Get yourself comfortable in that private place.
2. Make sure you have your book, journal notebook, a pen or pencil.
3. Like most people who try to share what is important, Jesus often spoke to those around him. His closest friends and followers often felt the Spirit of God in his words—even when they did not clearly understand their meaning. The Spirit of God in Jesus' words and actions is shared with us in the Gospels. Read the following account as found in Matthew's Gospel. Try

to hear both Jesus' words and the meaning behind them. Keep in mind the people who were originally listening to the words. Remember how well they knew this loving man. Reflect on what they knew about him by reputation as well as through personal experience.

> Jesus was still speaking to those who had gathered to hear his message. His mother and brothers came to the building, but they stood outside waiting to speak to him. Someone close to Jesus said, "Your mother and brothers are here, just outside the door. They want to speak to you."
> Jesus turned to the man who brought the message. He said, "Who is my mother? Who are my brothers?" He pointed to those gathered near to him and said, "Here are my mother and brothers. Whoever chooses to do the will of my Father in heaven, that person is my brother, my sister, my mother."
> (adapted from Matthew 12:46–50)

What you read was part of a dialogue.

After you have slowly read the Scripture dialogue, think about the meaning of Jesus' words. Some people choose to stay "hung up" on his referring to his brothers (a word often used in Scripture as we use the term *cousins*). Some have thought Jesus was rude not to run to his mother. Others have even suggested that his tone is disrespectful to his mother. But like Jesus' earlier listeners, people who believe know that this loving man was capable of neither disrespect nor rudeness.

In your journal, reflect on the above dialogue from Matthew's Gospel. Answer the question: What do Jesus' words and message mean to me today?

4. Go back in your journal and read what you wrote in answer to number 8 (page 86) in the last exercise.

5. List in your journal the names of all those who were involved in the incident you wrote about in exercise four (page 84).

6. Now create a dialogue for the same incident. In your wording, be as close as you can to what was said by you and the other person or persons involved. Spend no more than ten minutes writing. Write quickly and honestly. Say only what you think you said—not what you wish you said. Pretend you are merely a tape recorder.

7. Take a deep breath and relax.

8. Read what you wrote for number 6 above.

9. Now you are going to develop your dialogue. This time your dialogue will include not only the words, but the actions, and feelings of those involved. This is similar to what you did on page 75 in exercise two, numbers 5 and 6.

Take as much time as you need to write your dialogue.

Be as thorough as you can be.

Use the following forms whenever possible:

I said, _____.

When I said this, I felt _____.

What I meant was _____.

Then, __(name)__ said, _____.

Because that person felt _____.

What that person meant was _____.

Then that person (did) _____.

Then I (did) _____.

When I did this, I felt _____.

What I wanted was _____.

Then, __(name)__ (did) _____.

Because that person felt _____.

What the person wanted was _____.

As you write, it may be useful to look back to number 6.

10. After completing your dialogue, read what each person said, did, and felt.

11. Complete the following:

What I need to better understand the situation is _____.

The other people would have better understood if _____.

Something I understand now about the situation which I did not see before is _____.

12. In the opening reflection (number 3 above) Jesus said:

> Here are my mother and my brothers. Whoever chooses to do the will of my Father in heaven, that person is my brother, my sister, my mother.

Reflect for a while who gives you the most support to be you. After reading the following questions, answer each in your journal.

> Who understands you when few others do?
> Who stands by your side even when not agreeing with you?
> Who honestly tries to hear not only what you say, but what you mean?
> Whom can you be most honest with?
> Of whom can you ask a question and really want to hear the answer, even when you know you may disagree?
> Whom do you choose to support with your friendship and love?
> How do you show others who care for you that you care for them?
> Who will do something for you even when it is not easy?
> Whom will you lend a hand to even when you're already too busy?

13. Now close your journal. End your session with the following reflection by Saint Francis:

> Lord, make me a channel of your peace—that where there is hatred, I may bring love—that where there is wrong, I may bring the spirit of forgiveness—that where there is discord, I may bring harmony—that where there is error, I may bring truth—that where there is despair, I may bring hope—that where there are shadows, I may bring light—that where there is sadness, I may bring joy.
>
> Lord, grant that I may seek rather to comfort than to be comforted—to understand, than to be understood—to love, than to be loved.
>
> For it is by self-forgetting that I can find myself. It is by forgiving that I find forgiveness. It is in dying that I will awaken to eternal life.

Chapter 5
Automatic Writing

The notes of explanation for this chapter are included on page 98 in exercise two.

Exercise One

1. Relax in that special private place.
2. Make sure you have your book, journal notebook, a pen or pencil.
3. In Saint Paul's first letter to the people at Corinth, he speaks to a vision of life that sees

> 'things beyond our seeing, things far beyond our hearing, things beyond our wildest imagination, all prepared by God for those who love God'—things revealed to us through the Spirit.
>
> (adapted from 1 Corinthians 2:9–10)

To believe seems so foolish sometimes. When we are called to trust in God who we cannot see, and when we are certain we know what to do, it seems weak to ask for God's help. Somehow, we seem more able to pray when we need something we feel we cannot get on our own, or when we are confused or frightened or not knowing what to do.

If God's love can be there and be helpful in times of difficulty, isn't it logical to believe that such love is always available? If we can feel better about ourselves and our situation when we pray in difficult times, isn't it possible that regular prayer (even when we think we know best) to know God's will for us can be helpful?

There is strength in faith.

Reread the quote from Saint Paul in number 3 above.

Pray for the vision that Saint Paul speaks of. A simple "God, I'm doing my best, help me" (or the Serenity Prayer or a brief prayer of your choosing), repeated a few times, will help you be in a good frame of mind for this exercise. Repeat the brief prayer until you are very much at ease.

4. Start writing. Write whatever comes out of your mind, whatever comes through your pencil or pen. Write for twenty minutes. Write anything and everything that comes to mind. Hold nothing back. Don't worry about making sense, just write as much as you can in twenty minutes.

5. Reread the quote from Saint Paul in number 3 above. Repeat the "God, I'm doing my best, help me" prayer. Keep saying the words until you've blocked out of your mind almost everything you wrote for number 4 above.

6. Write for ten minutes. Just write whatever comes to mind. Be aware when you try to take control over the words. Stop. Keep writing. Don't try to make sense. Whenever you attempt to omit what comes to your mind, whenever you fear someone might see what you wrote, don't stop. Just keep writing. Write as much as you can in ten minutes. Start now.

7. Reread the quote from Saint Paul in number 3 above. Repeat the "God, I'm doing my best, help me" prayer. Keep saying the words until you are relaxed once more. Just try to let go and feel the joy of doing your best.

8. Start writing. Write for five minutes. Just let every word, every idea, every fantasy that comes to mind appear on the paper. Write as much as you can in five minutes.

9. Relax. Close your journal.

10. Stand up. Make sure your back, neck, and head form one straight line. Your arms should be at your side. Close your eyes.

   With your eyes closed, and without moving, think about the parts of your body. Without touching yourself, feel each part in your mind.

start with the toes
the tops of the feet
the balls or bottoms of the feet
the ankles
the shins
the hamstrings
the knees
the thighs
the pelvis
the waist
the upper torso
the chest
the fingers
tops of hands
palms
wrists
lower arm
elbow
upper arm
shoulder
neck
face
mouth
cheeks
nose
eyes
forehead
ears
hair

With your eyes still closed, bring your hands together in front of you, palms together in
"prayer" form. As you bring your hands together, say *Amen* and open your eyes. Drop your
hands to your side. This is the end of the
prayer-reflection.

Exercise Two

What you did in exercise one and will continue to do throughout this chapter is called *automatic writing*. It is a way to let your mind travel freely. With no controls over your mind, your pen or pencil can tell you things about yourself that you may never have imagined. The words you write may reveal secrets or at least hidden thoughts that might have stayed hidden or buried in the back of your mind.

One student said that while doing automatic writing she discovered some deep feelings about her boyfriend that greatly surprised her:

> **I went out with him because a lot of other girls wished they could ... not because I really respect or admire or even love him.**

On reading his automatic writing, a nineteen-year-old man who was getting ready to join the service had to reconsider his decision:

> **I'm very proud to serve my country. I do believe in the basic freedoms that we claim to be inalienable rights—life, liberty, and the pursuit of happiness. I do want the peoples of the world to respect one another. And I am certainly against any form of government that denies these rights to anyone. But doesn't war, by its very nature, require that we deny one person's rights for the protection of another point of view? Is war really the only way to**

> protect basic human rights? Does someone always have to be right and another wrong? It seems to me that sharing and caring count more than fighting.

Another young person who was on her way to college in six months thought she had it all together. She was planning to become a nurse. She seemed thrilled with the idea, and all those closest to her thought she would be happy.

> If I could do anything???? Well, that's a big measure. First of all, liberation or no, women cannot do everything. Society just isn't ready. Can you imagine me in television broadcasting? Yes, as a matter of fact. I'd be great. I like to be up front. I am good at making things look good even when they aren't—I've even convinced myself I could settle for being a nurse, and everyone thinks that I'd be just great. But the things that would make me a good nurse also could make me a good person for television broadcasting . . .

Automatic writing can be practiced regularly. You may find it helpful to work a brief period of five minutes into your daily journal plan. Try to keep it not more than five minutes. For one thing, you may be overwhelmed by too much material when you review your journal. In the long run, too much material can discourage you from writing.

1. Relax in that special private place.
2. Make sure you have your book, journal note-book, a pen or pencil.
3. At one point in the story of the birth of Jesus and his early childhood, the Scriptures intro-duce us to a holy man named Simeon. In the Scripture story, Simeon is a very old man. He apparently has spent a good part of his life in prayerfulness. His one great hope has been to live to see the fulfillment of the promises in the Old Testament. Even in his old age, his strong faith has given him a youthful attitude that is well expressed in Robert Frost's words, "I have miles to go before I sleep."

And then Jesus enters his life.

Now read his response to discovering in a young child named Jesus the hope promised him by his faith:

> Now, Lord, you may dismiss your servant,
>   In peace as you have promised by your Word;
> For my eyes have seen your salvation,
>   Which you have set before all the nations,
> A light of revelation for all the world,
>   And the glory of those who believe in you.

(adapted from Luke 2:29–32)

When we let go and let God run the show, we can discover wonderful things about ourselves, others, the world, and God. Read what you wrote in your last automatic writing session. Think about one thing you learned about yourself. Thank God for that newfound knowledge. By saying the above Prayer of Simeon, ask God to help you use well the knowledge you develop about yourself.

4. There is a special tool that can be helpful in automatic writing. For our purposes, let's call this tool a *talk-out*. A talk-out is any conversation with a real or imaginary person in a real or imaginary setting that you create for your journal.

5. Using automatic writing, write a five-minute talk-out with your mother. First write something that you would like to say. Then write her response. Continue the imaginary conversation for five more minutes. Remember, it is an imaginary conversation. It isn't even necessary for your mother to be living with you for this talk-out to take place. She may have already died. The conversation can still take place. Write without stopping for ten minutes.

6. Now choose another person to have a talk-out with. Choose your father, a grandparent, or a long dead ancestor about whom you have heard a great deal. Spend no less than ten minutes.

7. As a final talk-out, try a conversation with one of your teachers, your pastor, or a friend. Spend no less than ten minutes.

8. Read what you wrote for numbers 5, 6, and 7 above.
9. Answer in your journal the following questions for each talk-out:
   What did you write that surprised you?
   Explain why you were surprised?
   What did you write that you wish you had not written?
   If you could change anything you wrote, what would you change?
   What did you learn about yourself that made you feel good?
10. Close this session with the simple prayer reflection in number 3 above.

Exercise Three

Talk-out works well with imaginary people and situations. This type of automatic writing gives you a chance to let your mind travel like a time machine. You can go back through history or forward into tomorrow. Being able to see the past and the future through your journal can help you enjoy today.

1. Relax in that special private place.
2. Make sure you have your book, journal notebook, a pen or pencil.
3. After Jesus died, two of his disciples were walking to the town of Emmaus. They were feeling confused and hurt. They felt deserted by their friend. They might have even felt the anger and pain most of us feel when a friend dies—anger at God for taking the friend and anger with the friend for not being there when needed. The Scripture story goes on to tell us that the risen Jesus drew near and walked along with them. Yet, somehow, they did not recognize Jesus. In a loving way, he explained to them the message of the Scriptures. They found that they felt comforted by this stranger, and they asked him to share their evening meal. It was only when Jesus broke bread with them that they recognized him. (See Luke 24: 15–29.)

   Like Simeon, the two disciples discovered God in a most unlikely way. Simeon saw a child who was to change the world. The disciples heard words of love and understanding from a stranger, only to discover Jesus breaking bread and giving it to them as he had done before.

In your journal, try to be open to whatever God enables you to see and hear. As an opening reflection, use the following words from Saint Luke:

> Stay with us. The day is almost over, and it is getting dark.

(Luke 24:29)

Try to walk with the Lord as you work on your journal.

4. Write a talk-out with a person you don't know. Choose some government official (president, world leader, senator, etc.), religious leader, sports personality, artist, or other public figure alive or from history. For your first fiction talk-out, you might want to consider someone such as Dorothy Day, Francis of Assisi, Eleanor Roosevelt, Martin Luther King, Cesar Chavez, Albert Einstein, Babe Ruth, or another historically important person. Choose one person and have a five-minute talk-out with that person. Say whatever you want. Ask whatever questions you want. Listen closely and write exactly what you think they would say. Write quickly. Write for no less than five minutes.

5. Now think over the above list of possible personalities and others who come to mind as being great or important people. Pick one person who you would like to be. Write that person's name

in your journal.

6. Write a talk-out with the person whose name you wrote in number 5 above. Write quickly. Listen closely and write exactly what you think they would say. Ask any questions you like. Say anything you'd like. Share with the person why you think she or he is a great person. Write for no less than ten minutes.

7. Read what you wrote for numbers 4 and 6 above.

8. Answer the following questions for number 6 above.

What is most likable about this person?

How are you like the person?

What did the person tell you that surprised you about them?

What did the person help you find out about yourself?

Why would you like to use this person as a model for your life?

What is the most important thing this person did?

What does that mean to you?

If you could learn one thing from this person, what might it be?

What could this person teach you about you?

9. Close your journal.

10. Love, real love, often surprises us. Romantic love is exciting, and its effects on us are visible— just look at the number of times people on TV and in the movies fall "in" and "out of" love.

Real love is surprising because it is hard work. Somehow, we rarely see it or praise it until long after it has done its work. Jesus for example loved in such a way that he lived a life of love. The people of his time didn't reward him, and few even followed him. Mary his mother showed great love by being herself and just living the life she felt she was called to by God.

Mother Teresa of Calcutta recently was awarded the Nobel Peace Prize for her great work with the poor, suffering, and homeless. Her acts of love were only noticed many years after they had been in progress. But even our busy world had to take notice. When praise started to come her way, she was surprised. "It's not me, it's Him," she said. "I'm doing His work—giving back His love." Just as the world was surprised by this woman who receives no pay for what she does, she too was surprised that to others it was such a great task. She does what she believes God calls her to do.

As a closing reflection, spend about five minutes telling your journal how you think you love. Just begin writing with the words, "Today I love by _____ ."

Exercise Four

"Talk-out" can be done with ideas. You can talk out a reflection or mediation on something you have read or heard about. A Bible passage, a quote from a book, a TV show or movie, lines from a song, a passage from the newspaper. Anything you experience.

1. Relax in that special private place.
2. Make sure you have your book, journal notebook, a pen or pencil.
3. For a quiet time of reflection, read what you wrote in your journal in response to number 10 (page 106) in the last exercise. After reading your response, carefully read and think about the following passage from Saint John's Gospel:

> I give you a new commandment. Love. Love one another; just as I have loved you. Just as I have loved you, you must love one another. By the love you show for one another, everyone will know that you are one of mine.
>
> (adapted from John 13: 34–35)

4. Try a talk-out with your body. Tell your body about how you feel today. Let your body share with you its feelings about the day. Write automatically. Let each part of your body talk with you. Take as much time as you wish.

107

5. Now try a talk-out with your room. Have all the things in your room tell you about how they feel. Let them tell you about how they feel about you, the other things in your room, the house, and others who visit your room. Write for ten minutes.

6. Choose your favorite possession—the one thing you like best. Have a talk-out with that thing. Let it speak to you about how it feels being special for you. Listen as it tells you about you. Find out how it gets along with the other things and people in your life. Let it talk with you for ten minutes. Write quickly and don't leave out a word it says.

7. Read what you wrote for numbers 4, 5, and 6 above.

8. Complete the following statements for each of the three exercises (4, 5, and 6 above).

   I am surprised at learning _____.
   This helped me learn that love _____.
   I like this because _____.
   I was not happy with _____.
   I think I would like to _____.
   I forgot to write _____.
   This talk-out helped _____.

9. Reread the quote from Saint John in number 3 above.

10. Write a talk-out about the quote. Begin with the line "Love is shown by _____ " After writing for about ten minutes, close your journal.

Chapter 6
Reviewing

A journal is more than a place to write. Your journal can be a place where you meet yourself, a place to learn, a place to revisit parts of your life. If you regularly look back over your journal, you may begin to see patterns.

Each chapter has provided tools to help you review the exercises and increase your understanding. In the Daily Journal Plan on page 117, we have included a series of statements to help you review daily.

People often let life happen to them. A journal writer is a person who works toward living a life in tune with her or his true nature. *A journal helps us to choose life.* The journal writer has a chance to speak, to hear his or her own words, to reflect on those words in order to find meaning and a new meaning in those words. *In journal writing we practice the art of words.* A person who keeps a journal takes time to listen to God in her or his life—through prayer and reflection. Journal prayer is an art. This art must be worked at. Just as Christianity is a religion of choice, of continuous effort, of work and pain—*the journal is prayer.* Not everything we learn through our journal makes us comfortable. More often than not what we see in our journal makes us uncomfortable. No one is called to follow Christ in comfort. No one is called to pray in comfort. Spirituality is a way of life: a spiritual journal is part of that life.

In keeping a spiritual journal we can experience art, prayer, and life. Your journal requires a special discipline; it is truly an art form. It is a technique for listening to God and therefore a genuine prayer form. It teaches us how we live and how to live.

In reviewing or rereading our journals, we do discover ourselves—yesterday, today, and tomorrow. However you review, the goal is not to build a big ego, but to find out who you are. Through regular review you can learn to develop your self and your understanding of God. This is a demanding goal. Aside from the built-in reviews in these exercises, it is good to revisit your journal regularly (once a month, once every three months). You will most likely be surprised and often delighted at what you learn. One of the things you may learn is that what you wrote as important for one reason is really important for another reason.

Below is an entry from the journal of a young man who thought the incident recorded showed something valuable about his personality. At the time he wrote it, he felt that it indicated what a fine businessman he was:

Bought a used car today. Chevy with the works. Been looking at it for some time and finally made the plunge. Salesman wanted $2295. I told him I'd go $2000 even. No way. I stuck to it. He came down to $2200. I upped to $2095. He called his boss over and told him how we'd gone so far. Boss said we're $100 apart so he'd come down to his final 2175. Nope and I hung tough, hinting I could go 2125. Big sport boss said he'd flip me for the odd 50. I had it, but what the hell. I told him he could afford to flip and I couldn't. I finally got it for 2125. I actually Jewed him down 170 bucks. I took nearly an hour but it was like making $170 an hour and that is damn good wages.

About two years after having made this entry, the journal writer was surprised to see what it really said about him. The fact that he had made a good bargain was not very important. The fact that he had used the expression "Jewed him down" told him something about himself. It pointed up an unnoticed prejudice about Jews, something he'd not been aware of in himself.

113

The expressions we use in recording how we feel often tell us a lot more than the words we write. *Pay attention to language* as you review. Pay attention, too, not so much to the contents of the journal entries but to *your relationship* to what you write. Not what happened, or even what you said (though this is important also), but *what you feel about what happened and what you feel about what you said.*

The particular way of reviewing your journal is best left up to you. However, it should be obvious by now that the best way to begin is after a period of quiet and prayer for God's assistance. And never forget that the purpose of the review portion of the journal exercise is to locate goals for yourself and to boost yourself in the direction of those goals.

Ira Progoff, an expert on journal keeping, says in his book, *At a Journal Workshop,* that journal keeping is for discovery, not for proof for "your way." The journal is a source of growth, not a platform for standing still or being right. Progoff warns that journals are not meant to protect us against questions we do not wish to face; instead, they are tools for helping us meet the questions of our lives—of finding out what life means to us.

Journal keeping, then, will not only allow you to keep a written record, it will also aid you in making choices. Journal keeping can assist you in seeing possibilities, choices—some of which you would not even have been aware of without your journal.

We need to be careful to try to become aware of the meanings of what we have done and what we have thought. We need also to try to recognize how we either failed in doing or thinking about something, or how we chose not to do or think about something. When you made this choice, what other choice did you close out? Why? As you look back, did you make the best choice?

There are patterns to look for when we revisit our journals. Perhaps you discover that you became almost physically ill before every examination at school (or after each time you cheated on a test). What does that say about you? You may see for the first time that your daydreaming, more than you realized, tells you something about your spiritual life.

You may recognize that the newspaper or magazine stories that fascinate you most have to do with crime or violence. Or it may dawn on you that you absolutely shy away from any story that is unpleasant or that makes life look dangerous and frightening. Again, you can learn something about yourself from this.

What about the recurring scenes or themes in your dreams? What are your dreams trying to tell you?

Another pattern to look for is to see which kinds of people keep reappearing in your journal. You may learn about who your real heroes are. You may have thought, for example, that rock stars or sports personalities were the people you admired most, when actually you had more respect for completely different types of people, but you somehow never faced up to that. The same can be true of fictional or historical characters. Which do you admire?

Which do you despise? What does this tell you about yourself?

Once you begin to regularly visit your journal in order to make these discoveries about yourself, you may well be on your way to becoming an even more complete human being. This can be a lifelong adventure into your inner spaces. Journal keeping can be a lifelong adventure in placing first things first in your life. Journal keeping can help you find God's life within you.

Chapter 7
Plans and Prayers

A Daily Journal Plan

1. Get yourself comfortable in your private place.
2. Make sure you have your book, journal note-book, a pen or pencil.
3. Open with a prayer or thought that reminds you that you are doing something for yourself and with your God (for example, the Serenity Prayer or one of those in the back of the book).
4. Spend five minutes in automatic writing.
5. Read what you wrote during your last session.
6. After you have read, complete the following statements, writing about three or four sentences for each:

> When I look at what I wrote, I am most pleased about _____.
> I would most like to change _____.
> I'm really glad that I wrote about _____.
> I forgot to write _____.

7. This is a good time to thank yourself and your God for helping you share yourself in your journal. A simple, "thank you for letting me be me" is a reminder of this special gift you give yourself which you call your journal.
8. Don't forget that each exercise is designed to help you get to know yourself and your world. Be as honest as you can today. Remember there are no perfect answers. There is only one perfect way to keep a journal, and that is honestly.
9. Now you are ready to write.

118

Prayer from Scripture and Tradition

The following are some prayers that come to us through Scripture and the traditions of the Church. Many of these prayers have been used for generations. They may help you find the words and peace you need.

Alleluia

Alleluia is a simple prayer found in the Psalms. It was carried over from the Jewish tradition to Christian prayer worship. Alleluia means "Praise the Lord!"

Amen

Amen is a simple prayer which says yes to God.

The Lord's Prayer

The Lord's Prayer or Our Father is probably the best known of all Christian Prayers. It is the way Jesus taught us to pray as found in Matthew 6:9–13 and Luke 11:2–4.

Our Father, who art in heaven
hallowed be thy name;
thy kingdom come;
thy will be done on earth as
it is in heaven.
Give us this day our daily bread;
and forgive us our trespasses
as we forgive those who trespass against us;
and lead us not into temptation,
but deliver us from evil.
For the kingdom, the power,
and the glory are yours,
now and forever.

The Doxology

This prayer is a simple prayer in praise of
the Trinity.
Glory be to the Father,
and to the Son,
and to the Holy Spirit.
As it was in the beginning,
is now, and ever shall be,
world without end.

Hail Mary

The basic words of the Hail Mary are found in
Luke's Gospel 1: 28, 42. It is a prayer we can use to
help us to be open to God's love.

Hail, Mary, full of grace,
the Lord is with you.
Blessed are you among women,
and blessed is the fruit of your womb, Jesus.
Holy Mary, Mother of God,
pray for us sinners,
now and at the hour of our death.

The Shema

The Shema is found in the book of Deuteronomy
6: 4–5. It is a simple statement of belief.

Hear, O Israel, the Lord is our God,
the Lord is one.
And you shall love the Lord your God
with all your heart
with all your soul
with all your might.

For Awareness of God's Presence

The following selections from the Old Testament tradition can be helpful in centering your attention. From Ecclesiastes 3 . . .

For everything there is a season,
  and a time for every matter under heaven:
A time to be born, and a time to die;
A time to plant, and a time to pluck up what
  is planted;
A time to kill, and a time to heal;
A time to break down, and a time to build up;
A time to weep, and a time to laugh,
A time to mourn, and a time to dance;
A time to cast away stones, and a time to
  gather stones together;
A time to embrace, and a time to refrain from
  embracing;
A time to seek, and a time to lose;
A time to keep, and a time to cast away;
A time to read, and a time to sew;
A time to keep silent, and a time to speak;
A time to love, and a time to hate;
A time for war, and a time for peace.

(Revised Standard Version)

From Jewish Prayer in The Talmud
O you who are at home deep in my heart
help me to join you deep in my heart

The Blessing of Aaron

A Prayer for yourself or for others. Found in the Book of Numbers 6: 24–26.

May the Lord bless and keep you;
the Lord make his face to shine upon you
and be gracious unto you;
The Lord lift up his countenance upon you
and give you peace.

The Song of Simeon

These words from Luke 2: 29–32, though words of the old man Simeon, are words of new hope.

Now, Lord, you may dismiss your servant,
   In peace as you have promised by your word:
For my eyes have seen your salvation,
   Which you have set before all the nations,
A light of revelation for all the world,
   And the glory of those who believe in you.

In Jesus' Spirit

Here are some words from the New Testament that share with us the spirit in which Jesus prayed.

Father, into your hands I commend my
spirit.

(adapted from Luke 23:46)

I thank you, Father, Lord of heaven and earth,
for hiding these things from the learned and
the wise, and revealing them to the simple.

(adapted from Luke 10:21)

Words of those who have come before us

Those who have come before us continue to share their experience, strength and hope.

Saint Augustine (5th century)

May it be enough for us to believe that the cause of all created things, in heaven and on earth, visible or invisible, is none other than the goodness of the Creator, who is the one and true God.

Byzantine Tradition (8th century)

You are the Good Shepherd; seek me, a lamb, and do not overlook me in my wanderings.

Byzantine Tradition (6th century)

Almighty God, to whom all hearts are open, all desires known, from whom no secrets are hidden, free the thoughts of our hearts.

Contemporary

Open our minds to the future, Lord, and do not let us despair. Open our hearts to whomever we meet on the way, and bring us, with all your creation, to the perfect fulfillment of our hopes.

Saint Francis of Assissi (12th century)

Lord, make me a channel of your peace—that where there is hatred, I may bring love—that where there is wrong, I may bring the spirit of forgiveness—that where there is discord, I may bring harmony—that where there is error, I may bring truth—that where there is despair, I may bring hope—that where there are shadows, I may bring light—that where there is sadness, I may bring joy.

Lord grant that I may seek rather to comfort than to be comforted—to understand, than to be understood—to love, than to be loved.

For it is by self-forgetting that I can find myself. It is by forgiving that I find forgiveness. It is in dying that I will awaken to eternal life.

Saint Francis de Sales (17th century)

When did God's love for you begin?
When God began to be God.
When did God begin to be God?
Never, for God has always been without beginning and without end, and so God has always loved you.

Saint Ignatius of Loyola (16th century)

Lord, I freely give all my freedom to you.
Take my memory, my intellect, and my entire will.
You have given me anything I am or have;
I give it all back to you to stand under your will alone.
Your love and your grace are enough for me;
I ask for nothing more.

A Monk (6th–8th centuries)

Direct our actions, we ask you, O Lord, by your inspiration, and further them with your continual help; that every prayer and work of ours may always begin from you and through you be brought to completion.

Saint Theresa of Avila (16th century)

God grant me the serenity
   To accept things I cannot change;
   To change the things I can; and,
   The wisdom to know the difference.

Saint Terese of Lisieux (19th century)

Just for today,
What does it matter, O Lord, if the future
is dark?
To pray now for tomorrow—I am not able.
Keep my heart only for today, give me only
your protection today,
Grant me your light—just for today.

From the Sarum Primer (16th century)

God be in my head
   and in my understanding.
God be in my eyes
   and in my looking.
God be in my mouth
   and in my speaking.
God be in my heart
   and in my thinking.

Breath Prayer, Mantra

These short prayers fit into the rhythm of our heart beat and breathing. Every breath is a gift from God. Heart or breath prayer enables us to be aware of the gift and the giver. The following are some examples of heart or breath prayer:

Praise the Lord!
I am loved.
Lord have mercy.
Christ have mercy.
My Lord and my God!
My God and my All!
Not my will, but yours!
Through him, with him, and in him.
Jesus, Healer, make me whole.
To you I turn over my spirit.

Some are a little longer:

All praise, honor, glory, to Jesus.
Jesus, meek and humble of heart, make my heart like your very own.
My God, unite all minds in truth and all hearts in love.

And finally the famous "Jesus Prayer" from Saint Luke's Gospel:

Lord Jesus, have mercy upon me, a sinner.

JOURNAL NOTES